Lines Underwater

A mermaid anthology

based on

the Poems Underwater project

and edited by

Laura Seymour and Kirsten Tambling

HOLD YOUR BREATH...

Welcome to *Lines Underwater*, an anthology of new poetry, prose, photography, film, sculpture, and song that re-envisions the mermaid in the twenty-first century. We think that this volume has created a new set of mermaid myths, involving (amongst other things) social media, military training pools, cosmetic surgery, and the present-day architecture of seaside promenades and metro stations.

This anthology is the end-point of a project that we two made in spring 2013, when we visited three places in southeast England linked to water mythology and wrote poetry under the water, drew pictures, and took photographs there. The three places we visited were St Michael's Well in Longstanton (a cramped and cold baptismal well that is said to be built on the site of a pagan water shrine), Orford Ness (a disused World War II ballistics testing site, where the Wild Man of Orford, a scaly merman, was captured by medieval fishermen), and the Thames and Medway Canal (the modern day site of the marriage of the Thames and Medway rivers, as described by the early modern poet Edmund Spenser). Additional visits to watery locations like Deptford Creek, and interviews with previous artists who have taken an interest in mermaid mythology—like the poet Susan Wicks, the composer   Leo Geyer, and the librettist Martin Kratz—have also informed our ideas.

However, we were mainly interested in what other people think of mermaid figures in the present day, and so we asked people to send us in submissions. The result is this collection of wonderful new works that you have in your hand. As you read through this book, if you are a smartphone user, simply scan the Quick Read codes that are scattered throughout the pages, which will link you to interpretations of the mermaid in the form of songs and film. Alternatively, you can find all of the audio-visual contributions to the project at www.youtube.com/user/PoemsUnderwater.

We hope that these beautiful works give you as much enjoyment as we took in putting the anthology together.

—KT and LS

Cover design and illustration © Kirsten Tambling.
Selection, introductions, and typesetting © Laura Seymour and Kirsten Tambling
All individual contributions remain © the contributors.
First published in 2013 by Poems Underwater / Tyburn Tree.
Printed and bound by 4edge, Hockley, Essex.
Typeset in Garamond.

William Kherbek	Mermaid Sestina	8
	Mermaid Haikus	9
Christopher Brown	Mer Bench	9
Rebecca Gethin	The Mermaid Chair	10
Tony Winn	The Mermaid	10
Katie Hale	Siren's Song	11
Andrew Howell	Fisherman and Mermaid	12
C. R. Resetarits	Turbulence	13
Jennifer Brough	The Miracle Tin	13
Jeanette Stevenson	Underwater Garden	14
	Aquamaids Jaunt	14
Ieuan Edwards	My Underwater Love	17
Sara Eliot	Velvet Skies	17
Cheri Allcock	The Pool	18
Agnes Marton	Saraswati	18
Piotr Cieplak	#mermaidsrock	19
Karen Tang	Siren Stephen and his Mirror	21
Kirsten Tambling	Fish Tails	24
Sarah McKee	Wish You Weren't	27
Sue Wood	Postcard: "Salt Marsh with Cows"	28
Christopher Mulrooney	the city beneath the ocean	28
Nicola Moorhouse	Current	29
	Toroidal Vortices	29
Cheri Allcock	O	29
Phoebe Power	Stella's Body	30
Sue Wood	Becoming Sand	30
Polly Atkin	Lake Fever	31
Andrew Souter	Mermaid Tattoo	31
Bernd Sauermann	The Give and Take	32
Kate Noakes	Melusine at Châtelet	32
Ron Carey	Carrownlisheen	33
Michele Brenton	Spartia at Dusk	33
Charlotte Higgins	Ariel	34
Claire Trévien	Dahut	35
Luciana Francis	Canto Para Sereias	35
Marie Naughton	My Father's People	36
Adam Steiner	Angelic, Adrift	39
Sarah McKee	Miranda	40
Hilary Hares	Spell for a Mummified Mermaid	40
Virginie Colline	Mermaids and Sea Horse	41
Debby Akam	Girlfish	41
Jo Stanley	Adaptation	42
Meredith Knowles	Casin Lake Turtle	45
Philip Burton	Mermentor	46
Christopher Mulrooney	bed of mermaids	46
Chelsea Cargill	Gold	47
Jessica Taylor	Lost Catch	48
Ella Risbridger	The Lesson	51

CHAPTER ONE
The stories of washed-up things

One of the most common mermaid myths is that, lacking human souls, mermaids turn into sea-froth when they die. It is this that drives on Hans Christian Andersen's Little Mermaid: unlike her Disney counterpart, an immortal soul is her main desire. After all, to turn into froth is as good as annihilation—like much of the debris washed up by the sea, froth and bubbles are transient, insignificant, and unsubstantial. The writers, artists, and singer-songwriter in this chapter turn this on its head and deal with the possible significance of froth and washed-up things.

Martin Kratz, the librettist for the 2012 opera *The Mermaid of Zennor*, told us how intrigued he was that the Starbucks logo is a melusine (a two-tailed mermaid), observing that it would be a shame 'if the idea of the mermaid has been reduced to nothing but a paper cup floating on the ocean'. Two of the works in this chapter deal with the way in which big Starbucks-style companies can symbolise the ecological anxiety generated by capitalist wastefulness—and, like Andersen, they bring the mermaid into the city. William Kherbek's sestina describes the 'airy latte of urban myth | perfection'. Christopher Brown's photograph shows a windy sea rendering a promenade in Geneva unwalkable; here, froth both clears and deposits litter—most prominently a coffee cup lid. Both works encapsulate the traditional idea of the dead mermaid as frothy detritus, and present-day worries about disposable consumer culture, in images of coffee and froth.

Jennifer Brough explores the idea that things thrown up by the sea are not only consumable but of momentous importance. She explores the repercussions of the fact that its less-than-human status makes the mermaid desired more—but also cared for less —than a human being. In her poem, the mermaid is an edible, cashable object whose demise at the hands of a fisherman is deeply regretted by the mackintoshed hunter who 'sobs into his gin'. Brough draws delicately on ideas of over-fishing: whereas he may have no moral qualms about trawling for as many fish as possible, catching just one mermaid, one almost-human being, is too much for the fisherman and puts him over quota.

The confrontations between sailors and mermaids in this chapter question our responsibility for each other. In Katie Hale's poem, it is the sailor whose life is not respected, whilst in C.R. Resetarits' gorgeous work, sailors see mermaids from afar: 'a shimmer of skin just beyond the reef', no being with whom they can connect face-to-face. In Tony Winn's song, a mermaid tries her darndest to reel in a sailor, with a surprising end.

Rebecca Gethin's piece shows how, against destructive and wasteful impulses, poetry can become a space for conservation. It preserves for the twenty-first century the ancient myth of the carved mermaid chair at Zennor, in Cornwall: the site of seduction between a mermaid and a sailor (juxtaposed here with a modern Mer Bench). Jeanette Stevenson's *Underwater Garden* may have arisen naturally, or may have been tended by underwater beings.

The poet Susan Wicks told us 'a high tide can leave all sorts of unsightly and/or precious stuff...—some of it unexpectedly valuable, some of it an encumbrance—some of it about love, and some of it about sex or betrayal'. In our own work, we found a plethora of debris thrown up by the sea, whose apparent insignificance gave it a strange power—from military debris at Orford Ness to mugs, toy dinosaurs, and mobile phones at Deptford Creek—perhaps best encapsulated by this single headphone: a modern twist to the idea of putting a shell to your ear and listening to the sea.

In Chapter One...

William Kherbek is Port Magazine's visual art critic. His writing features in publications from London gallery Arcadia Missa, including *How to Sleep Faster*. www.arcadiamissa.com, www.port-magazine.com.

Christopher Brown is a screenwriter, director, and lecturer. Recent projects are *Knockout* (Best Screenplay, London Independent Film Festival; Cordelia Award-Best UK Screenplay, BlueCat Contest, LA), and a short film, *Remission*, out this autumn. His photograph *Mer Bench* is on p.9.

Rebecca Gethin has authored two poetry collections, *River is the Plural of Rain* (Oversteps Books, 2009) and *A Handful of Water* (Cinnamon Press, 2013), and a novel, *Liar Dice* (Cinnamon Press, 2011).

Tony Winn performs in his one-man-show, *Singing in the Bath*, and more! www.tonywinn.org.uk.

Katie Hale founded poetry project [insert text here] (sic). Her poems have recently appeared in *Poetry Review*, *The Frogmore Papers*, and *Cadaverine*. www.noordinaryblog.wordpress.com.

Andrew Howell is an eclectic artist working in a number of different media including 3D art, oil painting, drawing, sketches and watercolours. www.monstieur.org. His drawing *Fisherman and Mermaid* is on p.12.

C.R. Resetarits' poetry appeared recently in *New Writing: The International Journal for the Practice and Theory of Creative Writing*. Her essay on Nathaniel Hawthorne, gender, and genre appears in *Literary Imagination*.

Jennifer Brough works in publishing, is usually reading, writing or baking and visiting the seaside. Currently piecing together all her ideas, some can be found at www.jenniferbrough.wordpress.com.

Jeanette Stevenson, as a swimmer in her youth, lolled and cavorted with seals and otters in the Pacific Ocean. The occasional glimpse of silver tailed mermaids was an ecstatic thrill. Her artworks *Underwater Garden* and *Aquamaids Jaunt* are on p.14.

William Kherbek

MERMAID SESTINA

As it must, begin with the sea,
begin with the spreading of the myth
like the chevron trailing a swan on the face
of a lake. Halfway into the exercise,
you can see the swirl of froth
along an out crop of rocks, and the scales

of real life drop, and the line defining scale
and flesh runs to blur. The sea
is full of tricks and enough dream froth
stirred to life like an airy latte of urban myth
perfection, but also, from half-cut memory, an exercise
in summoning back an old reflection from behind your face.

And so there is music to be faced,
fading from the major to the minor scale
familiar from the much thumbed book of exercises:
fragments of the slow bit, in Debussy's The Sea
you liked once but now can't stand. The myth
always eats the brief joy; the truth is just froth

on the cappuccino top. I remember early morning soap froth
shining on her body, postcard from a past life. Face
it: your life is a ruined building, and it's not wise to myth-
ologise any given moment. There would have been lime scale
on the tea kettle and mould dotting the ceiling. You see
things with the eyes you want to. Life is an exercise

in deceiving yourself. Life is an exercise
in repeating yourself. Philosophy runs dry, dogs froth
on the grass where you first kissed, not a sea-
change, but its transformed like the non-existent face
on Mars' surface, a wind washed it away, time-scale
is what turns a brave lie into a myth.

But who has loved anything but a myth?
And who hasn't felt that surging desire exercise
every cell and bone, that could turn blubber or scale
into wet flesh and auburn ribbons drifting in the froth
beside perfect pink shoulders, and her face
obscured but in memory enough to lure you into the sea

to sleep beside her until the sea
itself boils indifferently away to froth
and fog to push away daylight's unwelcome face.

MERMAID HAIKUS

Seashell white night sky;
Maine's phosphorescence washed up:
her feet could be fins.

Rainbow scales wove a
promise, but her aching legs
shaped it into truth.

Rebecca Gethin

THE MERMAID CHAIR

During Mattins he mended holed nets,
looped clove hitches into the twine
squaring out the rows of mesh.

Now and then he glanced at prayerful wings of terns
and heard oystercatchers join in the responses.
Turnstones beetled along the sand like choirboys

eyes bright as rosary beads. Later, he said
he'd prayed with a woman he saw
sitting alone on the rocks

confessing to a cormorant priest
drying his black habit in the wind.
Vicar assumed he must have communed

with an angel, asked him to carve what he'd seen
on the chair. Not being a godly man he shrugged,
chiselled out her form, rounding the curve

of belly button and fish-scaled tail—
the way her eyes asked a man with salt
under his nails to slip into the world beneath.

At St Senara's church in Zennor there is a fifteenth-century carving of a mermaid on a chair. St Senara herself is said to have arrived from Ireland in a barrel and pitched up on the coast of North Cornwall.

Tony Winn

The Mermaid

Katie Hale

SIREN'S SONG

They came out of the mist: the old,
the young, the in-between,
knuckles sore from rowing, palms
stinging from the brine. I'd seen

it all before. Even their faces
looked the same: their cheeks
sagging; foreheads pearled with sweat;
eyes darting at the squeak

of oars on rowlocks. Some were grey
with too much work and lack
of sleep. Some were burnt or blistered.
Some, when they pulled back

against the waves, made little moans
that made me think of men
dying on battlefields, and, on bending
forward, they cried again.

We couldn't help ourselves but sing.
To see men's faces lift,
and hope rekindle in their eyes—
who wouldn't give the gift

of music? They were like children.
With every note we gave
them, they blossomed, until they leapt
into the tender waves

to swim. The younger men laughed
and splashed each other. The old
murmured strange harmonies and talked
of home, till they shone cold

in the sunset. Their strokes turned weak.
We held them, one by one,
as their hearts slowed. Our tune grew soft
and sad. Then they were gone,

like notes passing. We watched them sink.
All sailors return to the sea.
The sun tips over the horizon,
darkness pulls in, and we

are silent. Waves hurl themselves at
the rocks, and the rocks outlast
them, because they know nothing else.
The ocean is dark and vast.

C.R. Resetarits

TURBULENCE

Lightening/thunder popping up from kernel clouds from shoreside blankets from summer stirred rumblings, simply told as solstice zeal keeps popping up from cool, wet sands from dry, grass dunes from dark, cool theaters from out of nowhere, simply told a shimmer of skin just beyond the reef, a song, or simply told the summer dream as saturated air hits saturated heat 40,000 feet or less along the brimming shores.

Jennifer Brough

THE MIRACLE TIN

Sea food salad from a miracle tin,
rich spoils of the day drape down from a nail,
the mackintoshed hunter sobs into his gin.

Morning bought waves of a sea spun by sin
pure as a prayer billow large dreamy sails.
Sea food salad from a miracle tin.

Hours drip. That's it! The emerald fin
affixed to a body, marble rock pale.
The mackintoshed hunter sobs into his gin.

Grabbing the big nets, he casts them straight in
dark sea foams and froths with a shrieking wail:
sea food salad from a miracle tin.

When heaved on the deck, there's blood on her skin,
he holds out a hand, but her lungs soon fail.
The mackintoshed hunter sobs into his gin.

He can't bear to toss her over the rim,
picks up a scourer to descale her tail,
sea food salad from a miracle tin
the mackintoshed hunter sobs into his gin.

CHAPTER TWO
Nets, nerves and wires

Nets and ropes are a major part of mermaid myth. Legend has it that in the twelfth century the 'Wild Man' of Orford was caught by chance in a fisherman's net, brought to Orford Castle (on the Suffolk coast) and tortured. Later, this 'merman'—who was said to be covered in scales—was taken out for a swim on the end of a rope, but he managed to escape back to the open sea. Nowadays the shingle at Orford Ness, a disused ballistics testing site covered in military debris, is like a giant body, electric wires scattered over it like exposed nerves splayed and stretched. In some versions of the story, the Wild Man returned to his captors, letting them torture him again: the prison had become 'home' for him. On our trip to Deptford Creek, we saw that the cage-like structures of the creek's abandoned shopping trolleys have become protective homes for young fish, allowing them to hide from bigger animals. Far from frustrating prisons, they are essential to maintain the fish population.

Ieuan Edwards' linocut *My Underwater Love*, accompanied on the page by Sara Eliot's fantastic love song *Velvet Skies*, portrays a cord (or, rather, a tube) that is helpful and liberating rather than constraining and hindering. The diver's breathing tubes enable them to stay underwater long enough to share a kiss with their underwater love.

When mermaids go on land, they lose their tails, but in many legends their new legs are uncomfortable and they continue to long for the sea. Andersen describes his Little Mermaid bathing her painful feet in cold sea-water to soothe them—a bodily memory of her fins. Kirsten Tambling's line drawings *Fish Tails* explore the idea of phantom nerves continuing to haunt the mermaid body like nervous wires.

Twenty-first century wirelessness looms large in Agnes Marton's poem *Saraswati* and Piotr Cieplak's short story *#mermaidsrock*. Marton's phrase 'googled away the waves' launches a beautiful play on the ideas of 'streaming' and open sources both watery and digital. In *#mermaidsrock*, Twitter provides the structure for a doomed teenage love affair. This world where devastating breakups, international wars, and magical curses (a recurring motif in mermaid legends) are induced wirelessly and from afar, highlights how political and erotic ties can be metaphorical as well as literal 'nets' in mermaid mythology.

Karen Tang's wiry sculpture *Siren Stephen and His Mirror* comments wonderfully, if indirectly, on another theme of *#mermaidsrock*: the mermaid's (or in this case merman's) vanity about his or her hair, well known for its power of entangling the hearts of sailors. Siren Stephen was inspired by observing vain siren-like men in night clubs, offering a present-day take on the medieval mermaid's emblematic mirror.

Cheri Allcock's poem *The Pool* encapsulates the themes of the chapter as a whole: a tour de force of the ribbony, the sinewy, the bendy, the drawn or dyed border, the meshy and the metaphorical political 'tie' to the land or sea.

In Chapter Two...

Ieuan Edwards reached an artistic impasse in 2012 and put away his paintbrushes, dusted down his lino tools and founded The Black Gold Press (www.blackgoldpress.co.uk). His linocuts display a fondness for the Expressionist roots of the medium. His linocut *My Underwater Love* appears on p.17.

Sara Eliot is a London-based poet & singer/songwriter. Her unique sound—soulful vocals with a raspy edge—harmony and a touch of Jazz—delivers smooth lyrical poetry.

Cheri Allcock graduated with a bachelor's degree in Art History & Fine Art from Goldsmiths College in London. She now lives and works in Cairo.

Agnes Marton's most recent publications include the award-winning *Estuary: a Confluence of Art and Poetry* (USA; editor and contributor); *Penning Perfumes, Binders Full of Women, Catechism: Poems for Pussy Riot* (UK); *Gateway* (USA); *For Rhino in the Shrinking World* (South Africa).

Piotr Cieplak writes stories and, sometimes, books. He was the 2010-11 recipient of the Harper-Wood Studentship for English Poetry and Literature at St John's College, Cambridge. He lives in London and has just finished a novel—*The Crying Room*.

Karen Tang is a London-based artist. She studied MFA Sculpture at the Slade and her work has been exhibited internationally. Tang's sculptures emphasise formal investigation and material processes, often referencing science, sci-fi, architecture, and the urban experience. www.karentang.co.uk. Her sculpture *Siren Stephen and His Mirror* appears on p.21.

Kirsten Tambling is one half of Poems Underwater. London-based, she also writes, draws, and takes photographs. Her drawing-series *Fish Tails* appears on p.24. www.kirstentambling.com.

Sara Eliot

VELVET SKIES

Cheri Allcock

THE POOL

Try the fleshy meshy tones, open cast knit and flexible bones. And to love a beige divine, finger printed chalk along a blush contour line. Mauve nettle ribbon tie like meshy shoelaces around the neck, taught as you like, but unable to do the deed - you'll need something thicker. As water soluable sheets grow dry fuchsia puddles, sugar lumps will settle on the sand. Candy stripes will blend, and you'll forget what its like to be frivolous. And now to impoverish the appetite. What is left but the large rectangle of a greyish hued flesh, economy is creativity she said. I want to dance the tingle tangle over the surface, opaque it is, but merely a mask which will not hold the weight. Shots of liquid! - Where do i look? Run around slipping, bottoms wahey, rescuing and gripping bobballs in the toes. Hundreds and thousands of speckles, stick to pondering dilluted whims. Wishy washy surfaces and political instability, incomprehension to an open intuitive field. What she said! Clinging sensitivities make you breath tainted air, purity shall not come to you until the day that you dive.

Agnes Marton

SARASWATI

googled away the waves
then flown adeep

gravel, cobble, granule, pebble

fleeting glimpse: a swan?

ruminatida, sparkling
acres and miles

sniffed in sediments
traced the proof

the source, you are the source

upstream, inseparable

#MERMAIDSROCK

They released storks from bags so that she could complete her life's list of observed birds. Her trusted if resentful servant was the one to untie the rope. When Princess Ana saw the tortured creatures desperately trying to spread their broken wings and falling from the sky like hail, she knew that she was just about done with birds.

"I don't like them," she announced.

"What is that, your grace?" Nicolas, the trusted if resentful servant, pretended not to hear.

"I said: I don't like them. Storks are rubbish. They are definitely NOT going on the list." She sighed. "Frankly, all the birds since hawks have been a complete disappointment. Maybe with the exception of thrushes, but I am suspicious they're not even birds. Do you know what I mean?"

"Yes, your grace. I recall you saying that they were too much like insects."

"Precisely. Anyway, I'm done with birds now. Those on the list can stay; the rest will have to go."

"What about all the species you haven't seen yet?"

"What about them?"

"Can they stay?"

"Are they on the list?"

"No."

"Well then."

Princess Ana, soon to turn fifteen, had been conducting a survey of creatures inhabiting her small but strategically advantageous kingdom ever since inheriting it almost a year ago—following a horrible accident which claimed her parents' lives, and that of her younger brother, Joseph. The survey had a simple aim. The creatures that were graceful in distress would be allowed to stay; the rest would have to go. "We can't have monstrosities such as hedgehogs wandering around willy-nilly; they are unsightly," she had once remarked. She thought she'd start with birds—her favourite animals—but now she was positively bored and ready to move on to something more exotic.

"Bring me some mermaids," she said to Nicolas.

"Mermaids?"

"Yes, mermaids. Do we have any? I have always thought they'd be rather delightful but have never seen one in the flesh."

"I'm sure we can get some mermaids if that's what your grace desires."

"Well it is." After a moment's pause she said: "Nicolas."

"Yes your highness?"

"Does my hair look lovely today?"

"Yes, it does. Particularly lovely."

"Take a photo of me, then."

Ana handed Nicolas her royal smartphone, with the family crest emblazoned on the pink cover in diamonds, and he took a photo.

"Excellent. Thanks. You can now get on with acquiring these mermaids."

"Certainly, your grace."

Ana jumped off the throne and ran to her bedroom. She had a good look at the photo Nicolas had taken and decided that her hair did indeed look lovely today. *I'm so doing it.* She tweeted it at Prince Frederick. The tweet read: 'long day deciding which animals to keep in kingdom #worksucks #underagesovereigns.' And then, almost immediately, she sent a private message to her best friend Amelie, who was noble but didn't have a kingdom of her own: 'I've totally done it. I messaged him.'

Prince Frederick was the only other child monarch on the continent. His father had been forced to abdicate after a scandal involving a stable boy (and, if one listened to the more vicious rumours, a horse) and the kingdom was given over to a Trusteeship of Elders, with the sixteen-year-old Frederick as its official head. Unlike Ana, he didn't actually have to do anything; just turn up at official fêtes a few times a year. Which was just as well. On top of being a child monarch he was also a global superstar, currently working on his third album. Ana, like most of the teenage girls in the world, was madly in love with Frederick. His posters covered the walls of her bedroom. Once, she even met him, when he came to give a concert in the capital—part of his world tour. She came down from the royal box to greet him but was so star-struck and in love that all she managed to say was a stupid hello. She cried over this missed opportunity for five weeks.

A quick Facebook check. Ever since she became a ruler, Ana had had to deal with a flurry of friend requests. She didn't want to accept or reject them without proper consideration, but looking at everyone's profile was seriously eating into her days. It even led her to create a new account, visible only to other monarchs and presidents, a sort of rulers' intranet. She logged on and scrolled down through the posts. A genocidal dictator from a country bordering hers had posted a photo. It was truly horrid. It showed a massacre site; one of many from his most recent campaign of terror. The photo was tagged: 'A day in the countryside. LOL.'

Ana knew that the dictator was a dangerous man, best not to be messed with, but she couldn't stand for such cruelty. She replied to the post: 'Seriously? Disgusting. Honestly, build a bridge and GET OVER IT.' She felt bad and guilty afterwards, but also convinced that she had done the right thing. Her advisers had warned her about engaging in any kind of dialogue with the despot but she would explain the circumstances to them. And anyway, they were only advisers, what could they know. She was Princess Ana, the Chosen One.

Just how could she get away with being so defiant? How could she take over a country, at the age of fifteen, and face no real opposition from the many groups and individuals who would have liked to see her family ousted from the seat of power once and for all? Well, the answer was quite simple. Ana was amazing at cursing. Even as a toddler she could put a curse on anyone she wanted to. Many of her nannies and their families had died horrible deaths. The cursing was also the reason why some would say that Ana was spoilt. When still alive, her parents had found it very difficult to refuse her anything, fearing that her retaliative curses would cause more havoc than giving in to her demands (which, if one is to be fair, had never been particularly excessive). Now that she felt the weight of responsibility on her shoulders, Ana was much more restrained with her cursing. In fact, she hadn't cursed anyone in years.

A few busy days passed, divided between the affairs of state and school. *Yawn.* But on

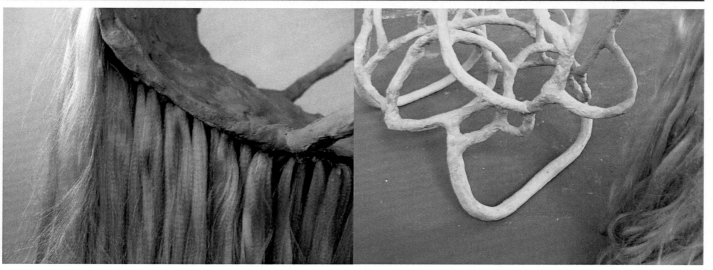

Nets, Nerves, Wires / Lines Underwater

Saturday morning Nicolas knocked on Ana's door at ten in the morning.

"I'm sorry to disturb your grace, but I just wanted to let you know that the mermaids are ready if you'd like to see them."

"Really?! How many?!"

"We have managed to capture four."

"Excellent!"

Still in her pyjamas, Princess Ana ran to the main hall of her palace and sat on her massive throne. She was very excited. She was expecting a sizeable tank to be rolled in. It would have to be big to accommodate four person-sized mermaids. She was certain that Nicolas would make sure they were comfortable and had plenty of space. So she was quite surprised when presented with a normal-sized fish-tank, if anything on the small side, brought in on an antique dresser.

"What is this?"

"The mermaids. We have three females and one male. I hope that's in order."

Ana got off her throne to get a better look. She had quite a shock. Now, it needs to be said that she'd had certain expectations about mermaids. Her mental image of the creatures had been shaped by Disney cartoons. Chiselled, pretty people with manes of hair and fish tails. These were tiny: the size of a seahorse. But the size wasn't the main problem. Ana wouldn't have minded miniature versions of what she had imagined. The problem was more, well, physiological. The mermaids were the other way round to what Ana had expected. They had the upper body of fish, and human legs (complete with tiny sets of genitals). They looked most peculiar.

"Uughh."

Ana recoiled at first, but couldn't stop looking.

"I guess it makes biological sense, right?"

"Absolutely, your majesty," said Nicolas.

"Can I hold one?"

"Of course—I am told they are quite friendly."

Ana put her hand into the tank and immediately all the mermaids started dancing merrily between her fingers. They brushed her skin with their fish faces, and tickled her with their comically fast-moving legs. They had, of course, no arms. Ana put the other hand in and scooped a mermaid out of the tank. She brought it close to her face to have a proper look. The mermaid seemed overjoyed. It might have even been smiling but it was hard to tell on account of the gills. It was circling and pirouetting in the cup of Ana's palms until it finally jumped out and gave Ana a fishy kiss.

"Oh I love them, Nicolas. I simply adore them."

First, Ana ordered tiny pieces of swimwear to be made for the mermaids – to protect their decency. Then, she spent days looking at the creatures and taking pictures of them. She was completely mesmerised. Until love came knocking at her door.

Prince Frederick replied to Ana's tweet from a few days ago ('Nice pic xx'— that's right TWO kisses). Not only that. He also liked her comment underneath the genocidal despot's picture. Apparently, he too was appalled by the atrocities. One message led to another, and all of a sudden Ana found herself conversing with Frederick. On Amelie's advice, she kept her cool; he was much more forward and liberal with the number of kisses after each message. Definitely very keen. He even claimed to remember Ana from their meeting after the concert. Their conversations were playful and flirty, but not childish. Frederick kept going on about the dictator and the atrocities. They really bothered him, or so it seemed.

Ana was in love, and bending over backwards to make herself seem interesting; mature for her age. But it was hard. She had so much on: the country had to be run, summer exams were approaching, and she had developed an obsession with mermaids which saw her staring at the tank for at least two hours a day. She didn't mention her fascination to Frederick, fearing that it would make her seem weird.

As is sadly often the case, soon the honeymoon was over.

After about a month of their online courtship, it was clear that Frederick was losing interest. Sometimes he would take as long as two days to reply to her tweets. Ana was beginning to despair so she turned to Amelie for advice. The dear friend got back to her almost immediately. Her wisdom was simple: 'Invade.' And Ana did.

To impress Frederick, and to show him that she too couldn't stand atrocities, Ana, overruling her most senior advisers, invaded the neighbouring country and deposed the genocidal despot. She did it the hard way; to prove that she meant business. She didn't use her cursing powers. It was a traditional invasion with armies and many dead. She even led her soldiers in battle, clad in pink Hello Kitty armour and riding a Shetland pony. It was over in a couple of weeks, with the dictator executed and a new transitional government installed.

Congratulations flowed in from all corners of the continent, but not a peep from Frederick. Again advised by wise Amelie, Ana kept her cool and waited for a week before making contact. It was agony. When she couldn't stand it any longer, she tweeted a photo of one of her mermaids at Frederick, saying: 'cute or what? #mermaidsrock.' Frederick got back to her almost immediately, no mention of the invasion. All he said was: 'What is that? #weird.' Not only that, he retweeted the picture to all his followers, all those teenage girls around the world who loved him, with a hashtag: #princessanasshittymermaids.

Dark despair began to reign in the Princess's young soul.

Not only was Ana's heart broken; she became the laughing stock of Frederick's more than one million Twitter followers. After she finished crying (three whole weeks of complete doom), she considered contacting Frederick to find out what had made him so unkind. Amelie said no. And then she added: 'You know what you have to do.' Ana reluctantly agreed.

She took a few days off to summon up her powers; she was very much out of practice. The next day, thousands of miles away, Frederick woke pretty desperate for water, with his little legs flapping around the enormous bed and his pretty heart-throb face covered in scales.

CHAPTER THREE
Bricked in and crossing borders

Mermaids are often frustrated: not at home in the sea (and falling in love with humans) but finding the land hostile. The Little Mermaid's legs come on condition of excrutiating earthly pain. The contributions to this chapter deal excitingly with living spaces, leaving homes, and submerged places.

Coastal erosion has created drowned villages all over the British Isles: Dunwich, Suffolk, was a thriving medieval city; today it is a tiny village whose remainder lies under the sea. Though scientists know Dunwich as a key site for underwater archaeology, folklore speaks more of its underwater church bells—as with many others said to be submerged around Britain, these are variously said to warn of storms, chime in Sunday sympathy, or sound in the ears of dying sailors.

Christopher Mulrooney's poem *the city beneath the ocean* relates the submerged dwelling to twenty-first century consumer culture, as the narratorial eye seeks 'a real estate sign' in the watery city. Claire Trévien's poem *Dahut* evokes the mythical city Ys in Brittany—the sound of its traditional 'bells that call us down' blending with the modern 'scrape of vinyl'. Luciana Francis' Portugese song was translated across the language-border especially for us: its English translation can be found on our website. Andrew Souter's *Mermaid Tattoo* fixates on markings lapped at by waves.

Much of the topography of today's rivers is determined by the urban built environment. In London, the river Fleet was forced underground by road building projects after the fire of 1666, whilst the Tyburn—namesake of the 'Tyburn Tree' public gallows—now flows through a shopping centre. Several of the works in this chapter describe the fusion of the mermaid's body with the present-day urban landscape: Kate Noakes' *Melusine at Châtelet* describes a woefully ignored mermaid bricked into a metro station; Phoebe Power's Stella cradles a swimming pool in her arms. Others deal with feeling out of place on land: the speaker in Sue Wood's *Postcard* is keenly aware of the absent sea, for example. Michele Brenton's photograph *Spartia at Dusk*, on the other hand, portrays a watery place and its human inhabitants from a 'mermaid's eye' view.

Nicola Moorhouse's paintings are designed to create a sense of 'immersion'. Deliberately excluding human and animal forms, her works invite the viewer to enter in to them and become the figure in her painting themselves. With them, as Ron Carey writes, you can 'open… the wavy roof | Of the ocean and slink… back to your own'.

In Chapter Three...

Sarah McKee's biography appears in the introduction to Chapter Four.

Sue Wood works as a creative writer in various health care situations. She is widely published in anthologies and journals. Her first collection *Imagine yourself as water* won a Cinnamon Press Award for Poetry.

Christopher Mulrooney's biography appears in the introduction to Chapter Four.

Nicola Moorhouse studied Visual Arts at the University of Gloucestershire. Her work focuses on the interaction of mind and body with nature. Her paintings *Current* and *Toroidal Vortices* appear on p. 29.

Cheri Allcock's biography appears in the introduction to Chapter Two.

Phoebe Power was an Eric Gregory Award winner in 2012 and a Foyle Young Poet in 2009. Her poems have appeared in *Magma*, *Cadaverine* and *Orbis*.

Polly Atkin's debut pamphlet *bone song* (Aussteiger, 2008) was shortlisted for the 2009 Michael Marks Pamphlet Award. Her pamphlet *Shadow Dispatches* (Seren, 2013) won the Mslexia Pamphlet Prize 2012.

Andrew Souter is a singer, guitarist, and songwriter from Wolverhampton. www.soundcloud.com/andrew-souter.

Bernd Sauermann's chapbook is *Diesel Generator* (Horse Less Press); a full-length collection, *Seven Notes of a Dead Man's Song*, is forthcoming from Mad Hat Press.

Kate Noakes is a Welsh poet. She lives mainly in Paris where she co-founded Paris Lit Up. Her most recent collection is *Cape Town* (Eyewear Publishing, 2012).

Ron Carey has been published in numerous journals and anthologies. He is studying for a Master's in Writing and working on his first poetry collection. *Carrownlisheen* was longlisted in the 2013 Gregory O Donoghue International Poetry Prize. www.roncareypoetry.com

Michele Brenton self-identified as a writer before she was five and now past fifty realises self-identification is a complex, never-ending journey of discovery and surprises. She is @banana_the_poet on Twitter. Her photograph *Spartia at Dusk* appears on p.33

Charlotte Higgins was a Foyle Young Poet of the Year Award and SLAMbassadors winner. Currently Young Poet in Residence at the Museum of Archeology and Anthropology in Cambridge. facebook.com/CharlotteHigginsPoetry.

Claire Trévien is an Anglo-Breton poet, the author of *Low-Tide Lottery* (Salt, 2011) and *The Shipwrecked House* (Penned in the Margins, 2013). She edits *Sabotage Reviews*, co-edits *Verse Kraken*, and co-organizes Penning Perfumes. www.clairetrevien.co.uk

Luciana Francis was born Luciana Saldanha in Sao Paulo, Brazil. Moved to London in 1998, where she still resides. Graduated in Anthropology & Media at Goldsmiths College. Currently writing a novella in her native Portuguese.

Marie Naughton won the 2012 Café Writers poetry competition. Her poems have appeared in magazines including *The Dark Horse* and *Crannog*. She is coming to the end of an MA in Creative Writing at the Centre for New Writing at Manchester University.

Sarah McKee

WISH YOU WEREN'T

Dearest though I suffer with the patience of Job here the coast's fringed with hermaphroditic seahorses Janus-headed myth-tailed biting stop you see there's more in of this world there's more to keep up here on the churning surface not yet not yet the next my treasured darling please STOP. Know that to my dearest love I bequeath a tickled trout: may the soft firm ink brown fish lie heavy in surprizèd hands. May every eye water at the sight of such scaly geometry. May my dearest love squeeze it gently so that he may die laughing. Meanwhile beloved I am not much longer for this world. It will be not much longer now. When I get to the underwater nunnery it will all be quiet, calm. There there's a gentian garden and small talk is unheard of. In recompense I offer ginger drops of sorry, cloudheight, acknowledge that I ought oftener to've worn slacks: insouciant hands in pockets and felt myself inelusively feminine. When I get me to the convent, 'maid tailed, it'll be as if some specific thing had never happened over & over. I'll be a well lost one, find a baseball mogul penpal at the bottom of a bottle and note there's a lick-stuck diamond stamp in the corner. In the box, from the chest, sorted. M'lud Narciss till then I'm terrified and rueful, la llorona, I go dragging the river with groan long fingers for my long gone children and I, for my long gone child self. There isn't a body to talk to. A list of persons of note is tucked under the fond octogenarian (Prospero)'s water-warped table: scribbles & scrawls look similar, so much the same it scares. One must love the bones and flesh enough so it (self-importance, personhood) is manifested thoroughly, re-superlative. My darling skeleton ah now I feel your marrow undeniably creeping back. For a time there was fish-for-brains in my bed folded in the herb and acid sleeping bag, cooking hot stuff oh yeah yeah yes. For that I gave the (single) tear, added salt to salt, stickily. 'm grown weary of trying all the time so hard to be a mensch, just keeping living on and on, turning over even the mossy stones, shaking the stickleback fish from the net. Scarcely joying in genitals or gentians or gentle abstractions, books about bones, frittering whatever time seems mine away as though hopeless and/or as though inevitable. What is it that you're too close to? Stein, you stand still! You're too close to the stone, too close to the stone shore to remember your proper, profound own, you are haunted by landly tenders who barely can fathom being lone. Beloved. We still shall be secretly connected through concealed analogy, through silverware, through abalone, we've rememorised enough to sustain us beyond Lethean dark. The mutual greed shall wane once I am submerged, once I am swallowed by this benevolent leviathan. Best love. Only recall sometime your unhappy clam: how we walked until our legs became brine, footfall faltered and we floated deep into the balmy night, the dark & plangent night, the close & troubled night, the sudden displaced night, the snow & salty night—how bridges shivered us into superstition—how words stuck in my gullet for your butter fingers to fish out. When I get me to the saline sub-stone nunnery, sweet-of-heart, when walking's quite done, when I close up far down below for good, you shall survive me like the early leg-growers, our ur-ancestors, mapless, guiltless evolutionaries, hobble-de-hoying onto the salted shore. Dearest. Yours.

Sue Wood

POSTCARD: "SALT MARSH WITH COWS"

White light and unentered ways
land of drain and fen
where angles lie level
clamped flat in their sea-memories.

The soil remembers shells, the current's dance
along its shifting spine
but here it skulks into land, quiet fertile land.

A few reeds sprout from rigid earth.
They are stiff, unbent in the silence
that brings report of restless shores and tides
beyond, beyond…

Winter birds speckle fields
fish the soil in grey fleets
while cloud merges with water
colourless, uncertain.

In this place of repeated lines
a distant hill startles itself.
There are no cows. There is no sea.

Christopher Mulrooney

THE CITY BENEATH THE OCEAN

it peeks along the edge of the waves
for a sign
a real estate sign
some order to cling to
an association or a party and doesn't care
all sold and carved up
distinguished by nothing save a very few airy bubbles

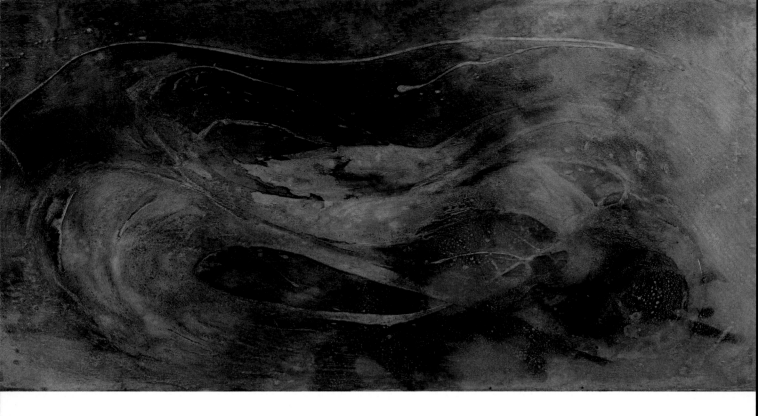

Cheri Allcock

O

You face me like an Atlas, broad and far in scope, distance, I can surely travel there. Sometime. Sometime soon? I'm seeing Hungary in your eyes now. And the baths of Budapest. Water baby, come with me. Lets go to one of the Poles. Or Poland? We can live an underground life in the kracks of… Moldova, up the river, down the path, of your nose. I know we will eventually. See eachother there. At the mouth.

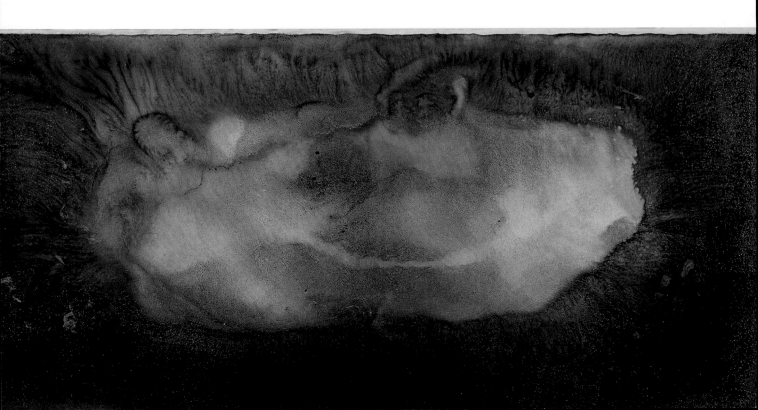

Phoebe Power

STELLA'S BODY

Her head's nothing expanse in the sea, calves
translucent airships. Ice-spikes ache from armpits,

coral in elbow-crooks, breaks in the lap
of wave silking her navel with jewels and scarves.

Salutis. Seas unscroll the globe as she wakes,
breasts hydrogen-bare, a zodiac belt. A face

so polished with kindness it could cut marble
to a round world, tile a swimming pool with soft arms.

Sue Wood

BECOMING SAND

Beach pebbles tongued, mouthed, sucked, spewn,
sit in the hand like gaudy sweets:
gob-stoppers stopped in banded reds,
barley twists fixed in agèd glass,
honey-combed calluses of brick,
a final sprinkle of old mortar.

Hold them—these are final things.
Beyond—the weary plod of dune
after dune, grain after grain.
Behind—the sea's mouth
savouring, hungering.

Polly Atkin

LAKE FEVER

'He, thus by feverish passion overcome …
Below him, in the bosom of the deep,
Saw mountains …'
Wordsworth, 'The Brothers'

That moment I was coming home to you
to my blue sky against your green slopes
blue-green iris of one great eye
dark wooded pupil.

It was only a photo I pitch-poled in to.
I was only the lateness of the hour the febrile
moths thup thup at the double-glazed window
at the back of my skull.

If you were a fever at sea I would dare
those mosses and ferns into ripples pitching
my whole life into the fiction and wake
mouth full of peaty freshwater clutching

shards of your inland shore. You don't
believe it? I nearly did it. I was
one foot in and sinking as in
deep black mud. I was hauling up

to dive or let go, and fall.

Andrew Souter

MERMAID TATTOO

Bricked in, crossing borders / Lines Underwater

Bernd Sauermann

THE GIVE AND TAKE

I offer you the selection of syllables to take as you
would directions to my house. I offer you "Portland,"
and I offer you "wings." I offer you "Boston," and I
offer you "legs." You offer me "Cleveland" and offer
me "shit" and the guilt of ever having spoken in the
first place, and you offer me the bright day an idea was
kicked around. You offer me a map of a streets laid
out as blue and twisted as the words of a stammered
lie. Anytown, America, slightly shaken with slender,
white hands.

Kate Noakes

MELUSINE AT CHÂTELET

A mirror-tiled morning, she's bare-tailed
in a métro tunnel, toes fused and splayed;

each foot a flipper displayed
to half a million passers-by, who fail

to see her in her damp, hair-tangled days,
but know they're off course from siren song.

Who will come now to carry her along,
to dive into the light of this wide bay?

Ron Carey

CARROWNLISHEEN

                    I am only beginning
To understand, floundering here, in this house, hard
Against the sea. Here, where we should have been
Breakfast for each other, you have left the kettle spitting
On the ring and, circling in a coral cup, tea—black as a bear.
You were not in your garden of shells—nor down
Where the strawberries nipple the cold Atlantic.
You are still not home when Morning shakes
The light-fingered leaves in the sticky hedge of maple
Where the hare hides her high, awkward feet.

                    Later, I'll go down
To that seaweed nest, where the rocks are as smooth
As dragon eggs, where the pounded spray scatters salt
On the skin you shed, where you opened the wavy roof
Of the ocean and slinked back to your own.

Charlotte Higgins

ARIEL

No one ever told you
that you cannot sing these new words
any more than a man can waltz on the surface of the sea

No one ever told you
that in this new language there is no poetry
that will fit in the shape of your lips

You see
this language has another word for beauty—
things don't sound this way where you come from—

So you stand in your fishnets and knife-edge heels
and you learn how to kiss with your new tongue
and they tell you you taste of salt
And they say
The women in our country do not talk this way

But no one ever said
that the language you'd known
that was easy as air, words tattooed on your bones,
the language as dark as the country you're from
would be uprooted, torn like a hook from your tongue

That new words would be sharper than you've ever known
would be bright as a pearl,
bright as sea foam.

Ariel is originally a performance poem—scan here for the audio

Claire Trévien

DAHUT

We know thunder isn't caused
by one cloud falling on another
or fire learning to speak
and choosing scorn
but the swallowing of Ys
under copper waves
and the appearance of your hair
out of the fold of history
icy like an unsalted road
with eyes too sunny for November
too snowy for March
and skin that seems to kiss
the fading of the dye
                    scrape of vinyl, scratch of sea
I follow the veins of your scent
here's where you buried a town
edited by fish into weeds
we believe in the bells
that call us down
deeper than textbooks
rummage
through volumes of backwash
for skin
                    scrape of vinyl, scratch of sea
There are enough wears in the tale to prove it
your locks clot the rocks
they wear it well

Luciana Francis

CANTO PARA SEREIAS

Marie Naughton

MY FATHER'S PEOPLE

I grew up supposing I was a land animal,
taught to swim badly
by my father;
he supposed he was the same.
Short of breath, prone to verrucas,
yet a whiff of chlorine,
filtered through bovril and cigarette smoke,
would soothe me like a lullaby.
I relish clearing drains, unblocking plugholes.
Culverts, sluice gates, sewage farms draw me,
any place where a current pulls
to a river or the sea.
I seek out derelict lidos, as tourists swarm
to the footings of Roman forts.
I know koi carp, tickle their bellies,
hand-feed pellets into their hosepipe mouths.
When the house is still
I trawl the internet for bell buoys—
Otter Point, Marblehead,
Ipswich Bay clang their call to prayer.
The webcam at Windermere
lets the lake
lap into the living room,
onto my green sofa.
Breast, crawl, back—my children were proficient
before the age of seven.
A smile brightened my father's face
as I huffed to the finish in Huron Basin.
Arthritis niggles in my ankles and knees
when I'm away from the pool.
Forest or ocean? the homeopath asks.
Jetties, piers, lighthouses summon me out beyond the edge
of human habitation.
Bleak by day, aglow by night,
viewed from a distance
by gulls, puffins, dolphins, seals.

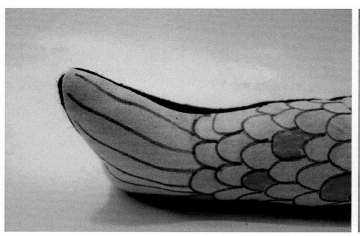
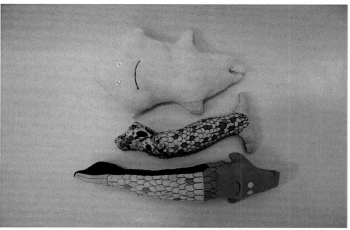

CHAPTER FOUR
Skin, Scales, Skirts

The works in this final chapter all look in different ways at vision, performativity, and transformation.

People tried for centuries to prove the existence of mermaids, or to capitalise on the idea that they might exist—in 1809 a respectable Scottish gentleman wrote a letter to the *Times* describing a mermaid encounter, which convinced no less a man than Sir Walter Scott. One of the stranger manifestations of this impulse to demonstrate was the 'Jenny Haniver', or mermaid fake. Supposedly made in Antwerp (whence the corruption 'Haniver'), in at least some proposed etymologies, Jenny Hanivers were named 'Jenny' as a way of gendering them explicitly female. But these were far from the Pre-Raphaelite vision of the mermaid bare-bosomed and beautiful: often, like Sarah McKee's Miranda or Hilary Hares' mermaid mummy, they were composites assembled from fish and monkeys or other humanoid animals, and people were known to flee from them in horror. As *Miranda* hints, Jenny Hanivers were generally more commercial ventures tapping into the freak show market than scientific objects in themselves—their creators (and presumably many other people along the chain) knew full well that they were fakes. Borne from port to port by sailors on trading ships, Jenny Hanivers were perhaps partly symbols of the capitalist process that saw people set out to sea in the first place, but also attempts to 'prove' through exhibition to a credulous audience that bizarre and composite sea-creatures did exist.

Similar commercial concerns governed the creation of Newton Perry's Weeki Wachee Springs in Florida, where beautiful women, hand-picked from all over the world, would 'play mermaid', in elaborate underwater theatres such as the one described in Chelsea Cargill's short story *Gold*. The straightforward, hyper-feminine performances of these American mermaids might call to mind other types of role-play and costuming—the 'pencil skirt of shot silk' in Philip Burton's *Mermentor*, which might just be a tail, or the performativity of gender roles—and even, perhaps, of humanity itself—as explored provocatively in Jo Stanley's *Adaptation*. Virginie Colline's concrete poem *Mermaids and Sea Horse* takes performativity to the poetic stage, with a work that is at once text and image.

Meanwhile, the 'regulation navy' recurring throughout Ella Risbridger's *The Lesson*, with which this anthology closes, might be uniform—homogenising, disguising —but also provides a context for exploration of another's body down to 'the muscle, and the bone'. The poem subtly evokes the emotional changes provoked by noticing the other's body in new ways.

Christopher Mulrooney's *bed of mermaids* sees its transformation facilitated through present day image technologies—an increase in saturation—while the hallucinogenic qualities of Adam Steiner's 'blues and greens' that 'weave a pitching sky|through the thick-lens of bobbing glass' evoke something of the colours and magic of the mythical mermaid.

In Chapter Four...

Adam Steiner is Deputy Editor of *HereComesEveryone* magazine. His first novel is *Politics of The Asylum*: www.silhouettepress.co.uk/politicsoftheasylum.

Sarah McKee lives near a lake in Berlin. She inhales an inordinate amount of live comedy. She keeps an irregularly tended blog: www.gormandgasp.tumblr.com.

Hilary Hares lives in Farnham, Surrey. She has a BA in Creative Writing and is currently working towards an MA in Poetry at Manchester Metropolitan University.

Virginie Colline is a French translator living in Paris. Her poems have appeared in *The Scrambler*, *Notes from the Gean*, *Prune Juice*, and *Frostwriting*, among others.

Debby Akam is a visual artist. *Girlfish* induces the ritualistic, meditative mechanisms of travelling between realms, and returning refreshed after connecting with Nature. More at www.debbygary.co.uk.

Philip Burton is widely published in literary magazines including *Stand*, *PN Review*, *Smiths Knoll*, *The London Magazine*, and in anthologies for children. www.philipburton.net.

Christopher Mulrooney has written poems in *Orbis*, *Weyfarers*, *Kaffeeklatsch*, *Crannog*, *Or*, *Pacific Review*, and *Otoliths*.

Jo Stanley is a creative historian who specialises in gender and the sea. She mainly writes non-fiction so this departure is a very satisfying pleasure to her. See www.jostanley.biz; www.genderedseas.blogspot.com.

Meredith Knowles was born in England but moved to the US two years ago. She now lives in Chicago, IL and takes photographs in her spare time. Her photograph *Casin Lake Turtle* appears on p.45.

Chelsea Cargill's creative nonfiction and poetry appears in several literary magazines such as *FuseLit*, *Duality* and *Spilt Milk*. Her fiction appears in the anthology *Shorelines*. See www.chelseacargill.wordpress.com.

Jessica Taylor is an artist and art psychotherapist. She works closely with notion that, within the process of creation, an emergence of the 'unthought known' is possible. www.jessicamaytaylor.co.uk. Her painting *Lost Catch* appears on p.47.

Ella Risbridger lives and writes in London, where she misses the sea and tends a windowsill garden. She is currently working on too many projects at once.

Adam Steiner

ANGELIC ADRIFT

Blues and greens
Weave a pitching sky
Through the thick-lens of bobbing glass
Bottled sun, full with life,
in the dusky, slurry dregs.

Twist-kick, changing tides
Shattered glass by surface smiles
Her first salt kiss, to rise above,
And see the other side.

Prickling-heat, the tight hinges of skin
She breathes the wash of bright squall
As white cries spiral down
A limping metal clang
Some juddering vault of fear.

Tangled lines, thump the dented boards
lashed kelp/bitten flesh/diamond slashed
Slapped down and panting flat
Her fused muscle flaps wildly.
Blunt wood tolls restless in palm
Ready to crack silvery skin
Draw back the slimed veil
Rainbow scales overtake milk-moon skin
Carved sharp in brittle daylight
Damned from the waist down.
But in the settled centre,
Her navel pool cradles life,
With glitters not gold.
Still and desperate, dark eyes reach to one side
Blinks damaged semaphore, untouched by grace.

Mutterings of low mercy
Stays the wood, by his side
Split the cords
Throw back the day's catch
And reel in the last nets.

Skin, Scales, Skirts / Lines Underwater

Sarah McKee

MIRANDA

Before I became a mermaid I had been a
smoking monkey. They shaved me & sewed
my torso onto a tail of faded blue
velvet, or vice versa. They rubbed
rouge onto my bare cheeks & mouth &
strung beads around my stringy neck.
The exhib. did not last because,
lacking formaldehyde or similar, they
displayed me in unclean water. I
puckered & shrivelled & stank & was
thrown to the ragged jaguar, who also
died soon afterwards. They stuffed him
& fixed his mouth wide & used his
tongue to catch ashes &c. I hope this
is helpful for your research.

       "Miranda"

POSTAGE PAID
To Whom it May Concern
Full Fathom 5

Hilary Hares

SPELL FOR A MUMMIFIED MERMAID

Tail of fish and eye of monkey,
grizzled snout and prickled chin.
Tang of toxic taxidermy,
touch of withered, shrunken skin.

Lure of ghoulish fascination—
mouth a grinning, rictus gash.
Cadaver of gross repulsion.
Abracadabra—splish, splosh, splash!

Virginie Colline

MERMAIDS AND SEA HORSE

Opaline dawn
mermaids fishing out suns
after the sea storm
a touch of
color
w
i
  t
   h
    a

      p
       i
        n
       c
      h

   o
   f

   s
    a
     l
      t

Debby Akam

GIRLFISH

Jo Stanley

ADAPTATION

Within a few weeks of my finally becoming 'his girl', the tasty WAG of a Formula One driver, it became knife time. I'd come from the Atlantic Rim area (somewhere that looks quite different on your maps to ours). Paul liked exotica and I was interested in speed and speed kings, that's why the Jetsetters Together agency matched us up. Mr Vroom Vroom and me, Ms Flip'n'Swish, that's what the receptionist joked. We'd agreed to meet first at the Brooklands Lake Manor Hotel near Silverstone. Over a lunch of sushi then pear our conversation was rich in talk of cornering, risking, winning and always propulsion, propulsion.

In our physical coupling later we'd got on as best we could, despite my impediment. It didn't restrict my sexual pleasure, certainly. People don't realise this about my kind but actually our clitorises are both accessible and well-developed; vaginas don't actually feel necessary to us, especially as we don't menstruate, children are born by another route, and most of us quite like oral sex. Paul, by contrast, was rather at a loss as to what to do.

Quite soon after we began dating he told me that he was revolted by women who don't depilate or who have pimples. For that reason, he objected to the skin on my lower body. So I paid to have a plastic surgeon excise the scales; each absence left a little ripple on my skin. Although I dutifully and daily covered the hundreds of small lateral scars with a heavy theatrical concealant I rather hated what had become of the surface. I kept all the redundant scales, in a jar in the fridge, so I could still admire what was left of the iridescence. Penny, our former cleaner, unfortunately discarded them last winter as the water looked so algaed; she'd thought it was some sort of mouldy holiday souvenir, like those bottles of vinegar with decorative fennel fronds waving in them. I felt I had somehow lost my brains, certainly my antennae.

The best thing about being at the Headley Court Private Hospital undergoing the process that the staff called the cosmetic removal of redundant extensions, was that I met Stella. An Afghanistan veteran, she used to be called Alan and now she was having her adam's apple pared down, as the first surgical stage of a process begun two years earlier with hormones. I hadn't realised till then that men's throats were so different to women's. We compared news of Leichner and Boots concealants; her scar, of course, was on more delicate skin. It was longer too, but at least there was only one of it.

Being a northerner Stella did good lugubrious gallows humour, so we often laughed at really the most awful things, that others would call bad taste: the savagery of the scalpel and its sometime slip-ups. We could contemplate anything. Any possibility in life. There was nothing in the world we couldn't say to each other. The difference between us was that Stella was feeling calm and satisfied that she was becoming more and more herself, as she said. Coming home. I, by contrast, seemed to be losing my sense of 'I'. 'Home' seemed to be a word I should look up in a dictionary; its meaning had become so fugitive to me.

As men do, Paul wanted that pleasure of plunging into my body. And in turn I did actually long for the ability to wrap myself round his trunk from both directions, not just surround him from one-or-other direction, which was all my existing lower limb enabled. (He had, I later discovered, been into women who had lost one leg. It was after meeting Heather Mills-McCartney. He joked that he was 'upgrading to two-legged chicks' with me.) Several of the other drivers had lost limbs in accidents on the track. So he was no stranger to radical surgery and nether absence. In fact, he was quite There-but-for-the–grace-of-God-ish.

And so we agreed that I would accept the knife, the severing; I would get two legs. Later an expert would fabricate that seemingly-crucial orifice at the top of them.

The question was how to cut and reshape. This was not a case of just calling in a skilled local woman of a relevant tribe to perform her familiar task like female circumcision: call it sex work. Nor was it anything like a fishmonger's simple filleting. Making functioning legs requires expertise, more like constructing part of the creature Mary Shelley's novel described. We considered using Max Revive, a taxidermist who'd worked with a Dutch museum on creating fake hybrids for a replica nineteenth-century wunder kammer. He had aesthetic cognizance of my ilk, though was rather too interested in how unlike a monkey or manatee I looked. But of course he knew nothing about how to enable muscular movement. Sirenomelia experts similarly didn't feel quite right to me; it seemed like a world too focussed on freak vs normal; I felt very normal and not at all aberrant. I was just rather ambitious for a change; I was taking my right to organise my body. Stella understood: "It just feels sensible to be helping myself turn at last into the me I properly ought to be…am," she nodded.

Finally a prosthetic limbs surgeon in a hospital for soldiers shattered by mines did all he could on the matter of viable legs for me. The amount of physio I have to do each day is tedious but initially I was helped by Paul's jokes about Bionic Women.

After that was done the next step was to find a cosmetics surgeon who would be able to manage the genital aspect of my conversion. Stella, who was now contemplating having surgery on what remained of her genitals after all that Oestrogen treatment had worked its wonders, put me in touch with Dr Wyman. Though well-known for her skill in helping former penises become vaginas, I was her first person who'd never had a penis in the first place. And it was in her South Kensington ward that I came to penetrability. Stella came to visit most days, not least because it was a way to familiarise herself with what might happen to her. Easily matey like so many soldiers are, she chatted to the transitioning people in the nearby bed—to an extent that made me irritable, as she was my only visitor. (Paul was trialling at Monza.) Most of the other patients predictably told her they were elated at reaching this stage of fulfilment of their dreams. But the suicide of her pal Esther after what Stella called the amputation of the remains of her meat and two veg was distressing her. As for me, my mood shifted, the more so as I looked at the ugly gash in the hand mirror and mourned the loss of my former inaccessibility. The operation was it seemed, only somewhat successful. It'll do, was the best that could be said. Dr Wyman apologised for her inadequacy. And I successfully dissuaded Paul from suing. The entire treatment, of course, took over eighteen months and swallowed a lot of Paul's earnings. But the day came at the Monaco Grand Prix when I could teeter with the best of the WAGs. You'd have thought I was just another blonde crippled—

seemingly—by her stiletto heels. You couldn't see the huge vertical scars under my sleek white trousers, the tiny ex-scale lines and this quarried place that is my fanny. I passed. Climbing up the podium to receive the silver cup, with Paul holding me at his other side like his other trophy, was tricky because my leg muscles are so poor (that's why we're living in a bungalow for now. No stairs). But I did it. I'd practiced for two months at the gym.

Then while he and the other Lotus boys partied I rested and waited for him to come home. We'd saved the first celebratory penetration for the night he won a major race. I tried to be on form for that, too. Really the nerve endings in my new walls weren't responding much and we were also discommoded by having forgotten to bring a tube of lube. The stress for both of us was, frankly, distracting. I wished he could appreciate clitorises more than he did; they're such a comfort.

And I have to say that from then on the relationship deteriorated. I tried to muster a sense of humour but being called 'Frankenstein' still undermined me. And I hated the way my difficulties in walking made me have to stay at home so much. Eventually I reverted to the mobility buggy I'd used before the operations. It assisted me in overcoming that worsening claustrophobia, that sense of the futility of my existence. All my changing, it was clear, was not making Paul love me more. Had I betrayed myself for nothing? I also found a volunteer driver, the kind who usually takes housebound people to stately homes and dentists. He had a Vivaro van big enough to take the buggy, but his favourite speed was 15mph. Between Bill and my buggy I started to learn to cope with a pace I'd never before conceived of. But often I wanted to screech at such slowness: it was such an end to my once-natural speediness.

Mainly I visited Stella, who was in supported housing in Slough. She was feeling lonely, for all that some of her army mates visited between tours. Seeing their injuries upset her but she loved feeling like one of the boys again, as they tried to drink themselves sane. Big Johnno, her best mate, had brought her a gift token for Ssh, the women's sex shop in Old Street. She offered it to me: "Wanna share it? We could get us semi-virgins a new vibrator each." No, it didn't seem to be what either of us wanted, actually. What did we want? "Intimate connecting of another kind?" I suggested. And really, that was what Johnno had just done: connected, deeply accepted. The token said that. But he'd only stayed an hour and half.

Looking back, I think I was probably suffering from that clinical depression so many people experience when they lose a body part. Some of my best friends were from a mastectomy group, Breastless Beauties, and very witty about it. However I felt the principal thing I'd lost had been my ability to use my element, water. I didn't actually feel I'd been deprived of any signifier of my femininity, as they did. But mourning is mourning, loss is loss; we were kin and they liked hearing my stories of back home.

After a while I realised that in following my path I'd actually volunteered myself for a form of Female Genital Mutilation. As a consequence I became something of a campaigner against the practice of FGM, especially the usual infibulation: the cutting off of all external genitalia and the stitching of vaginal orifices to enable male partners to enjoy penetrating a tight passage. I felt a kind of sisterhood after Paul began voicing his unhappiness with Dr Wyman's miscalculation of the girth he would require. "It's like mating with a slack old fish," he yelled one night. "Get an technician to reduce the diameter by twenty per cent or so! It's a bigger gauge than my exhaust pipe."

I don't really want any more surgery. Sometimes I consider returning to where I grew up. But having lost most of the means of sub-marine propulsion I would be, I think, quite immobilised there, as here. Once I attempted to swim in a hotel pool but felt shocked and humiliated at the lack of adeptness that besets me these days. Paul has occasional fantasies of being the father of a merbaby but I really can't face being still further adapted.

He had a tank of Koi carp installed, as an apology and sop. To help me feel at home, he says. The aquarium is the size of a modest cocktail cabinet; my Atlantic covers twenty-two per cent of the world's surface. Koi, he says, is a Japanese homophone for another word that means 'love,' but he didn't know what that other word was. Neither do I. Paul's mismatch of a present has, as you can imagine, led me to meditate much on the meaning of compatibility.

When he's away—yes, with new women, as well as on the race circuit—I watch a worn DVD Stella gave me of The Man Who Fell to Earth. 'It's about how the world can't respect us aliens,' she said. She's not listening to me very much just now as she's focused on the news that doctors can adapt a very sensitive clitoris indeed from her former penis. We joke about the multi-orgasmic future that could be in store... and I sometimes think I'd like to share it with her.

I still go the Dr Wyman's post-operative support group for people who've transitioned, although the others think that I don't really belong. I suppose they're right. 'But where do I belong?' I asked one day. Shrugging is what we do, a lot. Categories fail you. Maybe that's a kind of freedom.

Philip Burton

MERMENTOR

It touched the floor, her pencil skirt of shot silk.
Her hair, shinier than a wet cape, smelled of campion,
rocky thrift, newspaper ink, and Frosted sea-orache.
Late for your lesson, you'd deserve to be a whelk.
Her beguiling voice rippled like a bell of Damask sun.
The Welmar piano, a walnut cliff above an ivory wash

of waving notes; and above them—a white-sailed fleet
of paper music fluttered. Like a fish in a bowl
she was part of the room, never out or elsewhere.
Your scales are developing well, she'd assert.
I'd haunt a mirror, expecting my skin to unfold
lamina shields, but I stayed boringly inert.

Scales, in time, became arpeggios and fell from my eyes.
I was in the swim. Siren music fingered my heart.
My mermaid mentor grew serviceable feet
to demonstrate the pedals and collect her fees.
That was the day she said she must depart.
Along with me, from pier to pier, the ocean wept.

Christopher Mulrooney

BED OF MERMAIDS

they rolling in the current
as it passes above and below
trifling with their tresses
where the light is low
green very green
and still more green
to such a saturation

Chelsea Cargill

GOLD

It started first with imagining, which was the only real way to learn any trick. I had to say to myself *no-one is watching you*, since when I thought of the act all I could see was a sea of expectant faces staring at me through the glass and water. Under Mr McLelland's orders I started learning to hold my breath.

It wasn't true that no-one would be watching me, but this is what you had to believe. For instance, when you flew on a trapeze you had to be the only person in the world, Doris said. Actually hundreds of people would be watching, people with tickets who expected to see a mermaid. And there was Mr McLelland, who quickly flew into a rage when he felt the public had been let down.

I also had to tell myself, *you are not escaping a sinking ship.* Of course I wouldn't really be escaping a sinking ship, but every time I held my breath I kept thinking of passengers struggling underwater to free themselves from one. This started of course with news of the *Titanic,* which affected us all. For a time it was all we spoke about, and the tightrope walkers used nets at every altitude. Even the animals seemed jittery. Then we felt it was a jinx to mention it at all, long after the chimpanzees had calmed down. When I put my head underwater I could never hold my breath long enough to escape, and this was without having to flail about in the freezing currents or drag myself towards a lifebelt and be freed from fatal obstacles. My dress would be caught in ropes or dining room chairs, or a man would use me as a float to keep himself from drowning. We had heard of such stories from survivors in the newspapers.

"You don't need to swim, just float," Mr McLelland said in his sharp voice as he berated the elephant trainers for letting Elsie wander round town. They bowed and scraped in apology. "All you need to do is pose as a mermaid," he turned and said without roaring, an attempt at kindness. Meanwhile the seamstresses were busy putting the tail together from the fin upwards and discussing whether it had to be watertight, and if it needed scales. For a second Mr McLelland stared greedily across at the reptile cage before resuming his diatribe against the keepers. I decided to patrol the area regularly while I was in training and make sure none of the iguanas went missing. I didn't want any bloody patches of reptile skin to make an appearance on my tail.

After I'd practiced holding my head in the water barrel I went onto the river. It was freezing and I wore as many layers as I could fit into to keep warm, but this just seemed to make it worse afterwards when I ran back to our quarters and the wind felt like knives. I couldn't swim so found some reeds to hold onto and a place where you could climb down the rocks. The fact there was a strong current meant that the main focus was on not being pulled away. If I thought of the paying audience my eyes would start to bulge and my lungs would convulse. It was hard not to breathe in before I could claw my way back to the top. There were dangerous moments when I would drift away from my holding point and my legs would be pulled

downstream. It always ended with me splashing around like a half-drowned dog and having to lie on the bank until I'd finished retching. I would shiver all night.

"Imagine yourself as a bird," Doris would tell me as she put on her leotard and wing feathers. For her act she had to pretend it was natural to balance on one foot fifty feet in the air without thinking there was any possibility of falling. Still, I didn't think birds could survive underwater so I studied the seahorses hanging suspended in their glass case, and tried to imagine what it felt like to be a seahorse. Their movements were tiny and delicate, though every so often one would suddenly flick its tail and violent ripples would cough through the water. I wasn't sure why they suddenly took fright like this. I was worried that I would do the same and suddenly gulp water in the middle of the act and have to surface, or not be able to surface in time. I didn't put it past Mr McLelland to fill the case so full of water I couldn't take in air until the curtains closed. For him, maintaining the illusion was all that mattered, and if I drowned he would make up a cover story for the audience without blinking.

It just shows you, ladies and gentlemen, these creatures cannot live in captivity. Out of the sea they pine for their homeland, they refuse to eat! They die of mysterious causes, just like our sailors when they come into contact with them in their hiding places. Many men were sacrificed to bring to you this, one of the last wonders of our world...

I had even seen him wipe away real tears while committing some of the worst hoaxes. "This once beautiful half-lady, half-fish," he said when unveiling the previous mermaid, "is now reduced to a shadow of her former self." The mermaid was a a dried fish tail badly sewn to a shrivelled monkey and was so grotesque it made children scream. It was the kind of thing you found in the back rooms of freak shows all over the country. "Once she sang and played in the waves!" he lamented.

Doris told me she had met pearl divers when she had been in the Far East. Like most of her tales this was unlikely to be true, such as her rescue from a family of gypsies and the foreign-sounding accent she put on whenever any well-dressed men were near. Although it was possible she had met a real pearl diver as we did our annual circuit—or at least one that sold fake mermaids made from monkeys and fish tails.

"Your movements should be minimal," she said. "Like when you're looking through the water for pearls. You don't want to stir up the sediment on the ocean floor or disturb any sharks or octopuses."

"But Mr McLelland wants me to flick my tail around like a fish!" I protested. When he told me what my act would be he took me to watch the baby Beluga whale, one of his newest acquisitions. It didn't have much room to swim around but could change direction with an effortless swaying of fins. Its head was massive and it could only look at us with one eye at a time. *This is what I want*, he told me.

"Moving takes up more air," Doris said. "Maybe the river isn't the best place to practice. The bath is more realistic."

It didn't help my resolve when I heard they were going to make my viewing case into a shipwreck. Fake jewels were scattered on the bottom along with broken bits of wood and a tattered sail. My hair wasn't long enough to cover my top half so I had to wear a straggly wig that reached down to my belly. Its previous owner was the tattooed lady who used it to conceal the interlaced figures painted all over her legs, arms and back. It was most enticing when she revealed her secrets one by one, she said. The first time I tried it on she shot me a filthy look and told me she knew someone who had died from holding their breath. The hair smelled of sweat and stale beer.

"Mermaids are creatures of deceit," Mr McLelland said as if he were confiding in me. "They lure you in with promises of rubies and emeralds and then take you down to the depths of the ocean floor!" He raised his voice with the kind of drama usually reseverved for gathering crowds, which took me by surprise. It was true that several of the locals still believed in the existence of mermaids, or at least still spoke of them. Further north a notorious mermaid had taken jewels from shipwrecks in the Pentland Firth and used them to capture a sailor, who she then forever chained to the inside of her cave. Fisher folk always had a wry look when they told such stories but they all had unblinking eyes painted on the side of the boats, put there to ward off such creatures of misfortune. There were certain days when they wouldn't set sail even though there were clear skies and the seas were calm.

The tail was ready by the time I started training in the bath. It had been painted gold and I had to be sewn inside of it and then cut out afterwards. I wore the wig so I could get used to it fanning out underwater and practise ways of keeping my modesty, though Mr McLelland assured me that this definitely was not the purpose of the act. When I lay back the tail rested on the side like a beacon. I was completely unable to move my legs and so letting my face slip under the surface was always terrifying. Doris stood by to help haul me out when I signalled SOS. Then when I lay panting and holding onto the side for dear life some of the rousties would come and lift me clean from the water. Flecks of gold were left floating at the bottom.

Ella Risbridger

THE LESSON

And
          down, we went down, down together,
holding our hot breath together into the deep
end, all alive in regulation navy, holding hands
in regulation navy, down, down, I never went
so far down before, and my eyes were wide with
chlorine, stinging, but I didn't want to lose sight of you.
Underneath, you were all broken shapes in your regulation navy,
holding my hand, holding my breath,

and we wove our legs
together to one solid mass, to hold us down, down,
skin and skin and the grit on the tiles of the furthest
down, and by the black bars underwater we were
in our navy lycra and under my small hand all the fine hairs
on your back I had never seen above, and under the fine hairs
the skin, and under skin the muscle, and the bone;
under the water we were, under the water was the bone

and skin and muscle all together, of your hands and
my hands holding each other down and under the
regulation navy the skin and lungs, holding our breath
together, our hot breath together and hands together
and legs together in the chlorine water of the furthest
down, water and bone, skin and muscle, the sum of our
parts together down
and with our wrong hands, the hand not touching,
counting
          5
                    4
                         3
                              2
                                   1

to rise, and forget the simplest sum, the first lesson

(it seemed too soon to rise, but still we rose).

Skin, Scales, Skirts / Lines Underwater